DAILY CASH LOG BOOK

BOOK NO.:

CONTINUED FROM BOOK NO:

START DATE:

DEPARTMENT:

NAME:	
POSITION:	
ADDRESS:	
BUSINESS ADDRESS	
EMAIL	
TELEPHONE	
MOBILE	
FAX NUMBER	

NOTES

_____

_____

_____

_____

DAILY CASH LOG BOOK

DATE: FROM _____ TO _____   **PREV. BALANCE:** _____

DATE	DESCRIPTION	CASH IN	CASH OUT	BALANCE	COMMENTS
TOTAL					

DATE: _____   **SIGNED:** _____

DAILY CASH LOG BOOK

DATE: FROM   TO

PREV. BALANCE:

DATE	DESCRIPTION	CASH IN	CASH OUT	BALANCE	COMMENTS
TOTAL					

DATE:

SIGNED:

Daily Cash Log Book

DATE: FROM ___ TO ___   **PREY. BALANCE:** ___

DATE	DESCRIPTION	CASH IN	CASH OUT	BALANCE	COMMENTS
TOTAL					

DATE: ___   **SIGNED:** ___

Daily Cash Log Book

DATE: FROM ____ TO ____   PREY. BALANCE: ____

DATE	DESCRIPTION	CASH IN	CASH OUT	BALANCE	COMMENTS
TOTAL					

DATE: ____   SIGNED: ____

DAILY CASH LOG BOOK

DATE: FROM   TO

PREV. BALANCE:

DATE	DESCRIPTION	CASH IN	CASH OUT	BALANCE	COMMENTS
TOTAL					

DATE:

SIGNED:

DAILY CASH LOG BOOK

DATE: FROM   TO   **PREV. BALANCE:**

DATE	DESCRIPTION	CASH IN	CASH OUT	BALANCE	COMMENTS
TOTAL					

DATE: **SIGNED:**

DAILY CASH LOG BOOK

DATE: FROM _____ TO _____   PREV. BALANCE: _____

DATE	DESCRIPTION	CASH IN	CASH OUT	BALANCE	COMMENTS
TOTAL					

DATE: _____   SIGNED: _____

DAILY CASH LOG BOOK

DATE: FROM ____ TO ____

PREV. BALANCE: ____

DATE	DESCRIPTION	CASH IN	CASH OUT	BALANCE	COMMENTS
TOTAL					

DATE: ____

SIGNED: ____

Daily Cash Log Book

Date: From ___ To ___   **Prev. Balance:** ___

Date	Description	Cash in	Cash out	Balance	Comments
Total					

Date: ___   **Signed:** ___

DAILY CASH LOG BOOK

DATE: FROM   To   **PREY. BALANCE:**

DATE	DESCRIPTION	CASH IN	CASH OUT	BALANCE	COMMENTS
TOTAL					

DATE: **SIGNED:**

DAILY CASH LOG BOOK

DATE: FROM   TO   **PREV. BALANCE:**

DATE	DESCRIPTION	CASH IN	CASH OUT	BALANCE	COMMENTS
TOTAL					

DATE: **SIGNED:**

DAILY CASH LOG BOOK

DATE: FROM ____ TO ____   **PREV. BALANCE:** ____

DATE	DESCRIPTION	CASH IN	CASH OUT	BALANCE	COMMENTS
TOTAL					

DATE: ____   **SIGNED:** ____

DAILY CASH LOG BOOK

DATE: FROM   TO

PREV. BALANCE:

DATE	DESCRIPTION	CASH IN	CASH OUT	BALANCE	COMMENTS

TOTAL

DATE:

SIGNED:

DAILY CASH LOG BOOK

DATE: FROM _____ TO _____   PREV. BALANCE: _____

DATE	DESCRIPTION	CASH IN	CASH OUT	BALANCE	COMMENTS
TOTAL					

DATE: _____   SIGNED: _____

DAILY CASH LOG BOOK

DATE: FROM   TO   **PREV. BALANCE:**

DATE	DESCRIPTION	CASH IN	CASH OUT	BALANCE	COMMENTS
TOTAL					

DATE: **SIGNED:**

DAILY CASH LOG BOOK

PREY. BALANCE:

DATE	DESCRIPTION	CASH IN	CASH OUT	BALANCE	COMMENTS
TOTAL					

DATE:

SIGNED:

DAILY CASH LOG BOOK

DATE: FROM ___ TO ___   **PREV. BALANCE:** ___

DATE	DESCRIPTION	CASH IN	CASH OUT	BALANCE	COMMENTS
TOTAL					

DATE: ___   **SIGNED:** ___

DAILY CASH LOG BOOK

DATE: **FROM** **TO** **PREY. BALANCE:**

DATE	DESCRIPTION	CASH IN	CASH OUT	BALANCE	COMMENTS
TOTAL					

DATE: **SIGNED:**

DAILY CASH LOG BOOK

DATE: FROM _____ TO _____   **PREV. BALANCE:** _____

DATE	DESCRIPTION	CASH IN	CASH OUT	BALANCE	COMMENTS
TOTAL					

DATE: _____   **SIGNED:** _____

DAILY CASH LOG BOOK

DATE: FROM   TO   **PREV. BALANCE:**

DATE	DESCRIPTION	CASH IN	CASH OUT	BALANCE	COMMENTS
TOTAL					

DATE: **SIGNED:**

DAILY CASH LOG BOOK

DATE: FROM _____ TO _____   **PREV. BALANCE:** _____

DATE	DESCRIPTION	CASH IN	CASH OUT	BALANCE	COMMENTS
TOTAL					

DATE: _____   **SIGNED:** _____

DAILY CASH LOG BOOK

DATE: FROM TO

PREY. BALANCE:

DATE	DESCRIPTION	CASH IN	CASH OUT	BALANCE	COMMENTS
TOTAL					

DATE:

SIGNED:

Daily Cash Log Book

DATE: FROM   TO   **PREV. BALANCE:**

DATE	DESCRIPTION	CASH IN	CASH OUT	BALANCE	COMMENTS
TOTAL					

DATE: **SIGNED:**

DAILY CASH LOG BOOK

DATE: FROM   TO   **PREV. BALANCE:**

DATE	DESCRIPTION	CASH IN	CASH OUT	BALANCE	COMMENTS
TOTAL					

DATE: **SIGNED:**

DAILY CASH LOG BOOK

DATE: FROM   TO   PREV. BALANCE:

DATE	DESCRIPTION	CASH IN	CASH OUT	BALANCE	COMMENTS
TOTAL					

DATE: SIGNED:

DAILY CASH LOG BOOK

DATE: FROM   TO

PREY. BALANCE:

DATE	DESCRIPTION	CASH IN	CASH OUT	BALANCE	COMMENTS
TOTAL					

DATE:

SIGNED:

DAILY CASH LOG BOOK

DATE: FROM   TO

PREV. BALANCE:

DATE	DESCRIPTION	CASH IN	CASH OUT	BALANCE	COMMENTS
TOTAL					

DATE:

SIGNED:

DAILY CASH LOG BOOK

DATE: FROM   TO   **PREY. BALANCE:**

DATE	DESCRIPTION	CASH IN	CASH OUT	BALANCE	COMMENTS
TOTAL					

DATE: **SIGNED:**

DAILY CASH LOG BOOK

DATE: FROM ___ TO ___

PREV. BALANCE: ___

DATE	DESCRIPTION	CASH IN	CASH OUT	BALANCE	COMMENTS
	TOTAL				

DATE: ___

SIGNED: ___

DAILY CASH LOG BOOK

DATE: FROM ___ TO ___   PREV. BALANCE: ___

DATE	DESCRIPTION	CASH IN	CASH OUT	BALANCE	COMMENTS
TOTAL					

DATE: ___   SIGNED: ___

DAILY CASH LOG BOOK

DATE: FROM   TO   PREV. BALANCE:

DATE	DESCRIPTION	CASH IN	CASH OUT	BALANCE	COMMENTS
TOTAL					

DATE: SIGNED:

DAILY CASH LOG BOOK

DATE:

FROM   TO

PREV. BALANCE:

DATE	DESCRIPTION	CASH IN	CASH OUT	BALANCE	COMMENTS
TOTAL					

DATE:

SIGNED:

DAILY CASH LOG BOOK

DATE: FROM ____ TO ____   **PREV. BALANCE:** ____

DATE	DESCRIPTION	CASH IN	CASH OUT	BALANCE	COMMENTS
TOTAL					

DATE: ____   **SIGNED:** ____

DAILY CASH LOG BOOK

DATE: FROM ___ TO ___

PREY. BALANCE: ___

DATE	DESCRIPTION	CASH IN	CASH OUT	BALANCE	COMMENTS
TOTAL					

DATE: ___

SIGNED: ___

DAILY CASH LOG BOOK

DATE: FROM ___ TO ___   PREV. BALANCE: ___

DATE	DESCRIPTION	CASH IN	CASH OUT	BALANCE	COMMENTS
TOTAL					

DATE: ___   SIGNED: ___

DAILY CASH LOG BOOK

DATE: FROM ___ TO ___

PREV. BALANCE: ___

DATE	DESCRIPTION	CASH IN	CASH OUT	BALANCE	COMMENTS
TOTAL					

DATE: ___

SIGNED: ___

DAILY CASH LOG BOOK

DATE: FROM _____ TO _____ **PREV. BALANCE:** _____

DATE	DESCRIPTION	CASH IN	CASH OUT	BALANCE	COMMENTS
TOTAL					

DATE: _____ **SIGNED:** _____

Daily Cash Log Book

Date: From   To   **Prey. Balance:**

Date	Description	Cash in	Cash out	Balance	Comments
Total					

Date: **Signed:**

DAILY CASH LOG BOOK

DATE: FROM ___ TO ___   PREV. BALANCE: ___

DATE	DESCRIPTION	CASH IN	CASH OUT	BALANCE	COMMENTS
TOTAL					

DATE: ___   SIGNED: ___

DAILY CASH LOG BOOK

DATE: FROM   TO   PREV. BALANCE:

DATE	DESCRIPTION	CASH IN	CASH OUT	BALANCE	COMMENTS
TOTAL					

DATE: SIGNED:

DAILY CASH LOG BOOK

DATE: FROM ____ TO ____   PREV. BALANCE: ____

DATE	DESCRIPTION	CASH IN	CASH OUT	BALANCE	COMMENTS
TOTAL					

DATE: ____   SIGNED: ____

DAILY CASH LOG BOOK

DATE: FROM _____ TO _____   **PREV. BALANCE:** _____

DATE	DESCRIPTION	CASH IN	CASH OUT	BALANCE	COMMENTS
TOTAL					

DATE: _____   **SIGNED:** _____

Daily Cash Log Book

DATE: FROM _____ TO _____   **PREV. BALANCE:** _____

Date	Description	Cash in	Cash out	Balance	Comments
TOTAL					

DATE: _____   **SIGNED:** _____

Daily Cash Log Book

Date: From ____ To ____   **Prev. Balance:** ____

Date	Description	Cash in	Cash out	Balance	Comments
Total					

Date: ____   **Signed:** ____

DAILY CASH LOG BOOK

DATE: FROM ___ TO ___   PREV. BALANCE: ___

DATE	DESCRIPTION	CASH IN	CASH OUT	BALANCE	COMMENTS
TOTAL					

DATE: ___   SIGNED: ___

DAILY CASH LOG BOOK

DATE: FROM   TO   **PREY. BALANCE:**

DATE	DESCRIPTION	CASH IN	CASH OUT	BALANCE	COMMENTS
TOTAL					

DATE: **SIGNED:**

DAILY CASH LOG BOOK

DATE: FROM   TO   **PREV. BALANCE:**

DATE	DESCRIPTION	CASH IN	CASH OUT	BALANCE	COMMENTS
TOTAL					

DATE: **SIGNED:**

DAILY CASH LOG BOOK

DATE: FROM   TO

PREV. BALANCE:

DATE	DESCRIPTION	CASH IN	CASH OUT	BALANCE	COMMENTS
TOTAL					

DATE:

SIGNED:

DAILY CASH LOG BOOK

DATE: FROM   TO

PREV. BALANCE:

DATE	DESCRIPTION	CASH IN	CASH OUT	BALANCE	COMMENTS
TOTAL					

DATE:

SIGNED:

DAILY CASH LOG BOOK

DATE: FROM To

PREY. BALANCE:

DATE	DESCRIPTION	CASH IN	CASH OUT	BALANCE	COMMENTS
TOTAL					

DATE: **SIGNED:**

DAILY CASH LOG BOOK

DATE: FROM ___ TO ___   **PREV. BALANCE:** ___

DATE	DESCRIPTION	CASH IN	CASH OUT	BALANCE	COMMENTS
TOTAL					

DATE: ___   **SIGNED:** ___

DAILY CASH LOG BOOK

DATE: FROM   TO

PREY. BALANCE:

DATE	DESCRIPTION	CASH IN	CASH OUT	BALANCE	COMMENTS

TOTAL

DATE:

SIGNED:

Daily Cash Log Book

DATE: FROM ___ TO ___

PREY. BALANCE: ___

DATE	DESCRIPTION	CASH IN	CASH OUT	BALANCE	COMMENTS
TOTAL					

DATE: ___

SIGNED: ___

Daily Cash Log Book

DATE: FROM _____ TO _____

PREV. BALANCE: _____

Date	Description	Cash in	Cash out	Balance	Comments
Total					

DATE: _____

SIGNED: _____

DAILY CASH LOG BOOK

DATE: FROM   TO

PREY. BALANCE:

DATE	DESCRIPTION	CASH IN	CASH OUT	BALANCE	COMMENTS
TOTAL					

DATE:

SIGNED:

Daily Cash Log Book

Date: From ____ To ____   **Prev. Balance:** ____

Date	Description	Cash in	Cash out	Balance	Comments
Total					

Date: ____   **Signed:** ____

DAILY CASH LOG BOOK

DATE: FROM   TO   **PREV. BALANCE:**

DATE	DESCRIPTION	CASH IN	CASH OUT	BALANCE	COMMENTS
TOTAL					

DATE: **SIGNED:**

DAILY CASH LOG BOOK

DATE: FROM ___ TO ___   **PREV. BALANCE:** ___

DATE	DESCRIPTION	CASH IN	CASH OUT	BALANCE	COMMENTS
TOTAL					

DATE: ___   **SIGNED:** ___

DAILY CASH LOG BOOK

DATE: FROM ___ TO ___   **PREV. BALANCE:** ___

DATE	DESCRIPTION	CASH IN	CASH OUT	BALANCE	COMMENTS
TOTAL					

DATE: ___   **SIGNED:** ___

DAILY CASH LOG BOOK

DATE: FROM   TO

PREY. BALANCE:

DATE	DESCRIPTION	CASH IN	CASH OUT	BALANCE	COMMENTS
TOTAL					

DATE:

SIGNED:

DAILY CASH LOG BOOK

DATE: FROM   TO   **PREV. BALANCE:**

DATE	DESCRIPTION	CASH IN	CASH OUT	BALANCE	COMMENTS
TOTAL					

DATE: **SIGNED:**

DAILY CASH LOG BOOK

DATE: FROM   TO

PREV. BALANCE:

DATE	DESCRIPTION	CASH IN	CASH OUT	BALANCE	COMMENTS
TOTAL					

DATE:

SIGNED:

DAILY CASH LOG BOOK

DATE: FROM _____ TO _____   **PREV. BALANCE:** _____

DATE	DESCRIPTION	CASH IN	CASH OUT	BALANCE	COMMENTS
TOTAL					

DATE: _____   **SIGNED:** _____

DAILY CASH LOG BOOK

DATE: FROM   TO

PREY. BALANCE:

DATE	DESCRIPTION	CASH IN	CASH OUT	BALANCE	COMMENTS
TOTAL					

DATE:

SIGNED:

Daily Cash Log Book

DATE: FROM   To   **PREV. BALANCE:**

Date	Description	Cash in	Cash out	Balance	Comments
TOTAL					

DATE: **SIGNED:**

DAILY CASH LOG BOOK

DATE: FROM _____ TO _____   PREY. BALANCE: _____

DATE	DESCRIPTION	CASH IN	CASH OUT	BALANCE	COMMENTS
TOTAL					

DATE: _____   SIGNED: _____

DAILY CASH LOG BOOK

DATE: FROM   TO   **PREV. BALANCE:**

DATE	DESCRIPTION	CASH IN	CASH OUT	BALANCE	COMMENTS
TOTAL					

DATE: **SIGNED:**

Daily Cash Log Book

PREY. BALANCE:

DATE	DESCRIPTION	CASH IN	CASH OUT	BALANCE	COMMENTS
TOTAL					

DATE: SIGNED:

DAILY CASH LOG BOOK

DATE: FROM ____ TO ____   **PREY. BALANCE:** ____

DATE	DESCRIPTION	CASH IN	CASH OUT	BALANCE	COMMENTS
TOTAL					

DATE: ____   **SIGNED:** ____

Daily Cash Log Book

Date: From _____ To _____   **Prey. Balance:** _____

Date	Description	Cash In	Cash Out	Balance	Comments
Total					

Date: _____   **Signed:** _____

DAILY CASH LOG BOOK

DATE: FROM   TO   **PREV. BALANCE:**

DATE	DESCRIPTION	CASH IN	CASH OUT	BALANCE	COMMENTS
TOTAL					

DATE: **SIGNED:**

DAILY CASH LOG BOOK

DATE: FROM   TO

PREV. BALANCE:

DATE	DESCRIPTION	CASH IN	CASH OUT	BALANCE	COMMENTS
TOTAL					

DATE:

SIGNED:

DAILY CASH LOG BOOK

DATE: FROM ___ TO ___   **PREY. BALANCE:** ___

DATE	DESCRIPTION	CASH IN	CASH OUT	BALANCE	COMMENTS
TOTAL					

DATE: ___   **SIGNED:** ___

DAILY CASH LOG BOOK

DATE: FROM _____ TO _____   **PREV. BALANCE:** _____

DATE	DESCRIPTION	CASH IN	CASH OUT	BALANCE	COMMENTS
TOTAL					

DATE: _____   **SIGNED:** _____

DAILY CASH LOG BOOK

DATE: FROM _____ TO _____   PREV. BALANCE: _____

DATE	DESCRIPTION	CASH IN	CASH OUT	BALANCE	COMMENTS
TOTAL					

DATE: _____   SIGNED: _____

DAILY CASH LOG BOOK

DATE: FROM ___ TO ___   **PREY. BALANCE:** ___

DATE	DESCRIPTION	CASH IN	CASH OUT	BALANCE	COMMENTS
TOTAL					

DATE: ___   **SIGNED:** ___

DAILY CASH LOG BOOK

DATE: FROM   TO   PREY. BALANCE:

DATE	DESCRIPTION	CASH IN	CASH OUT	BALANCE	COMMENTS
TOTAL					

DATE: SIGNED:

Daily Cash Log Book

DATE: FROM _____ TO _____   **PREV. BALANCE:** _____

DATE	DESCRIPTION	CASH IN	CASH OUT	BALANCE	COMMENTS
TOTAL					

DATE: _____   **SIGNED:** _____

DAILY CASH LOG BOOK

DATE: FROM   TO   **PREY. BALANCE:**

DATE	DESCRIPTION	CASH IN	CASH OUT	BALANCE	COMMENTS
TOTAL					

DATE: **SIGNED:**

Daily Cash Log Book

DATE: FROM _____ TO _____   **PREV. BALANCE:** _____

DATE	DESCRIPTION	CASH IN	CASH OUT	BALANCE	COMMENTS
TOTAL					

DATE: _____   **SIGNED:** _____

DAILY CASH LOG BOOK

DATE: FROM   TO   **PREY. BALANCE:**

DATE	DESCRIPTION	CASH IN	CASH OUT	BALANCE	COMMENTS
TOTAL					

DATE: **SIGNED:**

DAILY CASH LOG BOOK

DATE: FROM   TO   **PREY. BALANCE:**

DATE	DESCRIPTION	CASH IN	CASH OUT	BALANCE	COMMENTS
TOTAL					

DATE: **SIGNED:**

Daily Cash Log Book

DATE: FROM ___ TO ___ **PREY. BALANCE:** ___

DATE	DESCRIPTION	CASH IN	CASH OUT	BALANCE	COMMENTS
TOTAL					

DATE: ___ **SIGNED:** ___

Daily Cash Log Book

DATE: FROM _____ TO _____   **PREV. BALANCE:** _____

DATE	DESCRIPTION	CASH IN	CASH OUT	BALANCE	COMMENTS
TOTAL					

DATE: _____   **SIGNED:** _____

DAILY CASH LOG BOOK

DATE: FROM ____ To ____   PREY. BALANCE: ____

DATE	DESCRIPTION	CASH IN	CASH OUT	BALANCE	COMMENTS
TOTAL					

DATE: ____   SIGNED: ____

DAILY CASH LOG BOOK

DATE: FROM   TO   **PREV. BALANCE:**

DATE	DESCRIPTION	CASH IN	CASH OUT	BALANCE	COMMENTS
TOTAL					

DATE: **SIGNED:**

Daily Cash Log Book

DATE: FROM _____ TO _____   PREY. BALANCE: _____

DATE	DESCRIPTION	CASH IN	CASH OUT	BALANCE	COMMENTS
TOTAL					

DATE: _____   SIGNED: _____

DAILY CASH LOG BOOK

DATE: FROM ___ TO ___   **PREV. BALANCE:** ___

DATE	DESCRIPTION	CASH IN	CASH OUT	BALANCE	COMMENTS
TOTAL					

DATE: ___   **SIGNED:** ___

DAILY CASH LOG BOOK

DATE: FROM ___ TO ___   **PREY. BALANCE:** ___

DATE	DESCRIPTION	CASH IN	CASH OUT	BALANCE	COMMENTS
TOTAL					

DATE: ___   **SIGNED:** ___

Daily Cash Log Book

Date: From _____ To _____   **Prev. Balance:** _____

Date	Description	Cash In	Cash Out	Balance	Comments
TOTAL					

Date: _____   **Signed:** _____

DAILY CASH LOG BOOK

DATE: FROM ___ TO ___   **PREV. BALANCE:** ___

DATE	DESCRIPTION	CASH IN	CASH OUT	BALANCE	COMMENTS
TOTAL					

DATE: ___   **SIGNED:** ___

DAILY CASH LOG BOOK

DATE: FROM   TO   **PREY. BALANCE:**

DATE	DESCRIPTION	CASH IN	CASH OUT	BALANCE	COMMENTS
TOTAL					

DATE: **SIGNED:**

Daily Cash Log Book

DATE: FROM ___ TO ___   PREY. BALANCE: ___

Date	Description	Cash in	Cash out	Balance	Comments
TOTAL					

DATE: ___   SIGNED: ___

Daily Cash Log Book

DATE: FROM ___ TO ___   **PREV. BALANCE:** ___

DATE	DESCRIPTION	CASH IN	CASH OUT	BALANCE	COMMENTS
TOTAL					

DATE: ___   **SIGNED:** ___

DAILY CASH LOG BOOK

DATE: FROM ___ To ___   **PREV. BALANCE:** ___

DATE	DESCRIPTION	CASH IN	CASH OUT	BALANCE	COMMENTS
TOTAL					

DATE: ___   **SIGNED:** ___

DAILY CASH LOG BOOK

DATE: FROM _____ TO _____   **PREY. BALANCE:** _____

DATE	DESCRIPTION	CASH IN	CASH OUT	BALANCE	COMMENTS
TOTAL					

DATE: _____   **SIGNED:** _____

Daily Cash Log Book

Date: From ___ To ___   **Prev. Balance:** ___

Date	Description	Cash in	Cash out	Balance	Comments
Total					

Date: ___   **Signed:** ___

Daily Cash Log Book

DATE: FROM _____ To _____   **PREV. BALANCE:** _____

DATE	DESCRIPTION	CASH IN	CASH OUT	BALANCE	COMMENTS
TOTAL					

DATE: _____   **SIGNED:** _____

DAILY CASH LOG BOOK

DATE: FROM   TO   **PREV. BALANCE:**

DATE	DESCRIPTION	CASH IN	CASH OUT	BALANCE	COMMENTS
TOTAL					

DATE: **SIGNED:**

DAILY CASH LOG BOOK

DATE: FROM   TO   PREY. BALANCE:

DATE	DESCRIPTION	CASH IN	CASH OUT	BALANCE	COMMENTS
TOTAL					

DATE: SIGNED:

DAILY CASH LOG BOOK

DATE: FROM _____ TO _____   **PREV. BALANCE:** _____

DATE	DESCRIPTION	CASH IN	CASH OUT	BALANCE	COMMENTS
TOTAL					

DATE: _____   **SIGNED:** _____

DAILY CASH LOG BOOK

DATE: FROM ___ TO ___   **PREY. BALANCE:** ___

DATE	DESCRIPTION	CASH IN	CASH OUT	BALANCE	COMMENTS
TOTAL					

DATE: ___   **SIGNED:** ___

DAILY CASH LOG BOOK

DATE: FROM _____ TO _____   **PREY. BALANCE:** _____

DATE	DESCRIPTION	CASH IN	CASH OUT	BALANCE	COMMENTS
TOTAL					

DATE: _____   **SIGNED:** _____

Daily Cash Log Book

DATE: FROM ____ TO ____   PREV. BALANCE: ____

DATE	DESCRIPTION	CASH IN	CASH OUT	BALANCE	COMMENTS
TOTAL					

DATE: ____   SIGNED: ____

DAILY CASH LOG BOOK

DATE: FROM   TO   **PREY. BALANCE:**

DATE	DESCRIPTION	CASH IN	CASH OUT	BALANCE	COMMENTS
TOTAL					

DATE: **SIGNED:**

DAILY CASH LOG BOOK

DATE: FROM   TO   **PREY. BALANCE:**

DATE	DESCRIPTION	CASH IN	CASH OUT	BALANCE	COMMENTS
TOTAL					

DATE: **SIGNED:**

DAILY CASH LOG BOOK

DATE: FROM ___ TO ___   PREY. BALANCE: ___

DATE	DESCRIPTION	CASH IN	CASH OUT	BALANCE	COMMENTS
TOTAL					

DATE: ___   SIGNED: ___

Daily Cash Log Book

DATE: FROM   TO   **PREY. BALANCE:**

DATE	DESCRIPTION	CASH IN	CASH OUT	BALANCE	COMMENTS
TOTAL					

DATE: **SIGNED:**

DAILY CASH LOG BOOK

DATE: FROM   TO

PREY. BALANCE:

DATE	DESCRIPTION	CASH IN	CASH OUT	BALANCE	COMMENTS
TOTAL					

DATE:

SIGNED:

DAILY CASH LOG BOOK

DATE: FROM _____ TO _____   **PREY. BALANCE:** _____

DATE	DESCRIPTION	CASH IN	CASH OUT	BALANCE	COMMENTS
TOTAL					

DATE: _____   **SIGNED:** _____

DAILY CASH LOG BOOK

DATE: FROM   TO   **PREV. BALANCE:**

DATE	DESCRIPTION	CASH IN	CASH OUT	BALANCE	COMMENTS
TOTAL					

DATE: **SIGNED:**

DAILY CASH LOG BOOK

DATE: FROM ___ TO ___ **PREY. BALANCE:** ___

DATE	DESCRIPTION	CASH IN	CASH OUT	BALANCE	COMMENTS
TOTAL					

DATE: ___ **SIGNED:** ___

DAILY CASH LOG BOOK

DATE: FROM ___ TO ___   **PREY. BALANCE:** ___

DATE	DESCRIPTION	CASH IN	CASH OUT	BALANCE	COMMENTS
TOTAL					

DATE: ___   **SIGNED:** ___

Daily Cash Log Book

DATE: FROM   To

PREY. BALANCE:

Date	Description	Cash in	Cash out	Balance	Comments
Total					

DATE: SIGNED:

DAILY CASH LOG BOOK

DATE: FROM   TO   **PREY. BALANCE:**

DATE	DESCRIPTION	CASH IN	CASH OUT	BALANCE	COMMENTS
TOTAL					

DATE: **SIGNED:**

DAILY CASH LOG BOOK

DATE: FROM To

PREV. BALANCE:

DATE	DESCRIPTION	CASH IN	CASH OUT	BALANCE	COMMENTS
TOTAL					

DATE: **SIGNED:**

DAILY CASH LOG BOOK

DATE: FROM TO   PREV. BALANCE:

DATE	DESCRIPTION	CASH IN	CASH OUT	BALANCE	COMMENTS
TOTAL					

DATE: SIGNED:

DAILY CASH LOG BOOK

DATE: FROM ___ TO ___   **PREV. BALANCE:** ___

DATE	DESCRIPTION	CASH IN	CASH OUT	BALANCE	COMMENTS

TOTAL ___ ___ ___

DATE: ___   **SIGNED:** ___

Hello,
Thank you so much for purchasing!
Without your voice we don't exist
Please, leave your opinion about this book

Thank you so much!

Made in the USA
Monee, IL
02 September 2021